IN THE WIND

ISBN: 979-8-9911983-9-4

Cover Photograph by Ed Ruzicka
Cover and Book Design by Alan Abrams

Sligo Creek Publishing Company
Silver Spring, Maryland
sligocreekpublishing.com

IN THE WIND

POEMS BY ED RUZICKA

SLIGO CREEK PUBLISHING COMPANY

This book is dedicated to my wife Renee Stickels-Ruzicka, whose gentle nature supports me in countless ways.

I want to thank Gary Beaumier, Jane Napolitano, Clare Imholtz and Michael Newell for their kind regards toward these poems as they came along. Every member of my writing group (Ben & Eileen Shieber, Andy King, Charles deGravelles, Carolyn Ricaptio, John Tarleton, Randolph Thomas, Marilyn Shapley, Jeanne George and Richard Kilbourne) helped these poems immeasurably.

I am also indebted to my insightful copy editor, Meg Freer.

Contents

*"I thought that we did not deserve to be in the world
if we did not see it."*

Earnest Hemingway, "True at First Light"

*"You can tell a story in no time,
but it is another matter to live one."*

Ralph Sneeden, "Evidence of Journey"

CONDORS IN THE ANDES

INCAN TRAIL

Aguas Calientes, Peru   July 1979

I

First day I plod, stumble up steeps
sometimes jagged as lightning.
Breath comes hard. Calves burn.
Exhausted, at four I turn back
to find level ground for my tent.

As I descend, the valley darkens.
Sky opens. A gang of condors
soars on curlicues of wind, pivot,
shoot off, rarely flex a wing.
Wind is a condor's toy.

II

The next morning, I abandon the path,
work down through vines, stones, scree,
and exotic broadleaf to reach a torrid stream.
I hop twice, sit cross-legged on a boulder
that parts white current to munch granola, banana.

The flames of orchids, mercurial birds,
trout fins, insects cut from gemstones all glint.
The stream swishes silver, claps and bells.

As I lurch back up to the trail,
a Dutchman approaches, stammers,
"Get out, quick. The guidebook says
the venomous Fer-de-Lance lurks there."
I halt, stand, forearms dusted with pollen.

Ice-white, the brook roars. Later
I begin to wonder, "Is there really no heaven
but heaven?" Only the quick-striking
Fer-de-Lance seems to say, "Yes."

III

I make Dead Woman's Pass under tender snow,
stumble onto a moonscape of basalt.
Dark clouds, furious, slung low,
pour in over a ridge. Lightning stabs.
When sleet slants in hard, I find
a craggy grotto deep enough
to cower dry. I nibble carrot,
burrow bone to rock.

Morning brings exultant blue.
Feet dance along thin shelves.
Below, the Urubamba River
thunders through rock. My bones
are the bones of a condor.

IV

On the third morning I descend ancient steps
into the Emperor's summer retreat
made of stone expertly chiseled and fit.
Earthquakes cannot take these walls apart.
Swallows weave above terraces.
Condors wheel. Far across the valley
a cataract tumbles inch-white.

That night I sleep beside the Urubamba
in a room with seven others, a hand-mirror,
a razor, and snow-lines in a *pensión*.
One is a traveler from Lisbon I met
weeks ago on the coast. Magdalena
must want to view Machu Picchu
from the glacial heights of cocaine lines.

Already the girl is too thin.
Later I will learn that Magdalena died
soon after at needle's end on a mattress
somewhere in the Imperial Valley.

For now, I take myself for a night soak.
Alone, exhausted, I give these bones up
to steaming mineral baths under a dark cliffside.
The Southern Cross has already started its icy arc.
I am over three thousand miles
from anything I have ever known.

WHAT IS STERLING, NOTHING MORE

Above Cochas Chico, Peru   June 1979

I

When I get above the tree line,
a torrent spews out of a cave mouth,
crashes down cliff-fall.

I make the sierra, its hip-high grasses,
spongy bogs. Three times I happen upon boulders
chiseled into rough altars where potatoes
are laid out to freeze at night, dry under sun.

There are thousands of varieties of potatoes in Peru,
some violet, others yellow as jasmine.
Spindly, ovoid, round, all feel good in the palm.

Finally, I reach a ridge, look back
at a parade of alpacas led by one man
who is the size of a leaf. Bells dangle
off the alpaca's necks, ting thin in thin air.

I swallow canteen water, drift
along a compass vector, close to sky,
upside down upon the world's vast ceiling.

II

I have walked away from the Altiplano
where families eke out a living

to go toward a site that has no face,
no desire, no compassion.
I stop by a lake, half-frozen, whey blue.

To the south lies an escarpment
covered with a rust-colored brush.
A half-mile east, sheer cliff-drop,
impassable. Behind me the west
is stone, wind and scrub. The north
– unknown, silent, boundless.

I lie down. I sleep. Before dawn
rings the mountains awake,
a snow goose honks four times.

LEONCIO

Cochas Chico, Peru   June 1979

In his courtyard, Leoncio Veli
carves stories into gourds.

At ten a.m. he etches a family of vicuna
that graze on a ridge. Sun arcs shadow around him

lean, then thick, then lean again.
His face is buffed bronze, marked, furrowed.

On the gourd sitting next to Leoncio
there is a band complete with bass, accordion and tuba.
Every day he wears the same trousers,
shirt, sweater, jacket, all colorless.

Leoncio adds tonal shade to his carvings
by rolling embers on a stick of ash over his etchings.

Two houses down, his brother does the same.
It is painstaking work, done slowly.
Leoncio is as quiet as his mountain.

THRESHING

Cochas Chico, Peru   July 1979

Leoncio wakes me before six
to march down to the next town.
I am to drive the Datsun
that is kept there in a cousin's garage.
I have been trying to teach Leoncio how to drive
but it is terrifying. He uses the gas
more than the brake. Sheep, alpaca,
old men, children, chickens
have to scurry and dive off the road.

This morning so many of Leoncio's family
pile onto, lean off, the pickup's bed
that I can't see out the rearview.
On a great knoll overlooking the Juaja valley
everyone whips out machetes, sets to hacking wheat.
They gather cut stalks, bundle them,
spread them out across hand-woven blankets.

With gestures, they tell me to drive back and forth
over the blankets. That is how they plan to strip
chaff from grain. I tell them it is not clean.
They laugh with the sun in their mouths.

They raise grain, let chaff and seed sift down
in a golden rain. "*Limpio, muy limpio,*"
To keep the herd at bay, women and children
pluck up dried dung, zing it at cows.
I try to explain microbiology in a language
I can barely use to order lunch. "*Limpio,*" they sing.

The Datsun jolts back and forth.
At noon we drink cool *maté* from clay jars.
By sundown we have a harvest of bronze pyramids.
On the way home slumping figures bounce over ruts.
I drop them off. Guided by starlight,
I squeeze the Datsun back into the garage.

Silent, exhausted, Leoncio and I
trudge back up the side of the mountain
with legs as heavy as stone.

THE DUTCH GIRL

Atalaya, Peru   August 1979

Determined to see Amazonian jungle
I go over the Andes in a cargo plane
that touches down on a grass air strip.
I walk the single stripe of street
straight to the single hotel.

At the hotel bar, a squad
of Peruvian marines adopts me.
The marines have flown in
to recover the body of a Dutch girl
who drowned in the Tambo.

For three days these marines
take me out in a powerboat,
dive into every conceivable snarl
of the Tambo's treacherous surges.
Somewhere in the Tambo
a graduate student from Ghent
has gone grey under a current.

Late afternoons we venture to pubs
or pad, towel over shoulder,
through jungle tangle
to a jade pool under a waterfall.

On the fourth morning,
I wake up with yellow eyes.
On the seventh I catch a flight
out to Lima where MDs
can properly treat jaundice

and leave behind
a group of men grown restless
as fish continue to disrobe
and enjoy the Dutch girl.

Two Fail a Test in Humanity

Bogota, Columbia   May 1979

Boeing tires touch the tarmac after midnight.
I hook up with two Germans and a Stanford Grad student
who is coming back to Bogota to see her grandparents.

Elise says it is too late to wake the old folks.
We pile into a cab that shoots through red lights.
Streets are dim. Curs wander.
Gangs of urchins dart into alleyways
or lean and shiver beside brick walls.

One after another, hotels turn us away.
Streets are empty. The city is full.
Finally Elise relents, dials her grandparents.

Their house is perched on a mountainside.
Goats chew cud in a moonless fog.
The door is unlocked. Her grandparents
have gone back to sleep. They have
left cookies, plates, glasses, a pitcher of milk.

Every guidebook says to avoid milk
unless you are certain it is pasteurized.
The Germans leave their glasses
sitting out untouched. I drink deep
as an animal at a trough. The milk is cool.
The next morning Elise tells us that her grandparents
have a stainless steel machine in their barn
that pasteurizes milk in less than two hours.

Having just taken innumerable pointless tests
to earn a Master's degree, it feels good
to have trusted these two sweater-wrapped,
wizened, arthritic and relentlessly kind grandparents
and to have passed my first real exam.

A Beer in Quito

Ecuador May1979

I

On a bus to Cali that takes blind turns
at breakneck speeds, I meet a cook from Boston
who keeps a three-day Bogie beard.
James is cut from old cloth,
knows the ropes of travel, Gringo style.

I go to the sea at Esmeraldes.
On the second day, I grab branches,
pull myself up a steep cliff. At the crest
iguanas big and slender as bicycles
crash away in all directions,
fling themselves downward over bush tops.

For a few minutes there is nothing but sun.
Then pelicans start to dive out of clouds,
corkscrew, splash into the Pacific's crazed blue foil.

They gobble so fast, I can't fathom what fish they eat.
One after the other, the pelicans shoot one limb out,
lift a second wing from sea-jangle. Saltwater runs off
as they skim waves, rise into an orange sun.

They dive again. Merrily, in rhythm
with wind and sea, the pelicans dive again.
I tell myself I will stay in South America
until all the money runs out.

II

 Back in Quito I bump into James at the P.O.
Though the sun is already low in the west,
we decide to grab a beer on a pub patio.

This guy, James Joyce – no kidding,
that is his God-given name –
has been on the trail since early March.
"This is all I wanted.," James Joyce says.
"This is what I came for, to have a beer in Quito."

We watch old men in a park step, stoop,
roll bocci balls. Above them, palms
flush tangerine. Our *cervezas*
are dark and cold and good.
In strips of slant light
the bocce players seem slender.

COTOPAXI

"Most of Ecuador's land mass has been formed by the eruptions of a series of highly active volcanoes." – Stephen Edwards

In open air a matriarch leans over a cauldron.
Her black turban surrounds a furrowed, pecan face.
Her multitude of necklaces jabber light and gem
over a backdrop of the valley's floor.

When she stands, the wattle and daub hut behind her
stands out. Her burgundy shawl backs the necklaces.
Once she had more teeth. Chickens peck the yard.

Listen, where arable, patchwork steeps tumble
toward the valley floor, a river sounds.
On the bus out of Quito I smell papaya, cheese,
live chickens in burlap bags, urine. I see
a distant ridge where the river's source
cascades ice-white. Wind whips
clouds into a furious surf.

Snow shrouded, Cotopaxi breaks above
regal as any phallus head. It appears before us,
then follows behind for over a hundred miles.
Cotopaxi is the father of all that I see.

AGUAS CALIENTES

Banos, Ecuador   June 1979

A subterranean current passes over lava,
seeps through fissures in rock, gathers
in steaming pools. I sink down, stew.

Twenty feet away, an icy stream rips over rock.
A French girl teaches me to go back and forth –
icy cold then the brink of intolerable heat.

In the stream, I crouch under boulders.
Fistfuls of water pound my back.
I ease down into the steaming bath.
Back and forth. "You have had enough,
Mr. American Man?" the French girl asks.

Delirious with pain and relief, I close my eyelids.
Arms drift, loose as jellyfish tentacles.
In a landscape rimmed by mountains,
laced with the flight of crows, eagles
my body is as pierced and exquisite

as St. Sebastian's body (he martyred,
pinned by arrows, me punctured by needles of heat)
at the instant he gave himself into the arms of seraphim.

MORNING IN COCHAS

Cochas Chico, Peru June 1979

In Peru I lived with an artisan's family.
He had traveled to Colorado for an International
Gourd Competition. Had been treated royally.
So wouldn't let me pay a single Sol
for the adobe room off the courtyard
where I stayed for two months.

Sometimes I'd wake in the middle of the night
to the sound of rushing water and know that
someone had opened an irrigation gateway,
let water flood down through a small canal
on the side of the street. There was an elaborate
labyrinth of cuts woven over the hillside. Elders,
my host among them, met weekly in a shaded cantina
to work out what was fair with their resources.

Leoncio and I gave each other language lessons
every morning. *"Gato"*, he'd say and "meow."
His favorite was when I helped him enunciate,
"See you later, alligator." He always ended with,
"Entonces, vamos." which seemed to mean – as we
have come to this mutual point of satisfaction, it is time for
us to part. Not merely, "Well then, let's go."

Mostly Leoncio sat on courtyard concrete. Moved hourly to
stay in sun as he carved and burned illustrations into gourds
that he purchased once a year from a town on the Peruvian
coast. His cousin drove him there in the only truck owned in
Cochas Chico. It was kept in a garage in another town a mile
down the mountain. This was Leoncio's Datson but he didn't
know how to drive. I was teaching him that.

Early mornings when we were still in the shade of mountains, I would hear Leoncio and his wife through the wall as they talked in a patient way my parents never had. A way I couldn't get to with either of my two wives, only rarely reach now with Renee, believe that my daughters have already found. Leoncio's voice was restful, a rumbling that penetrated earth. Hers was contoured.

Came in whisks, soft pools, ripples.

NINETEEN MINUTES

Cerro Jallacate, Viscas, Peru   May 1979

I cut across a slope.
On a meadow a woman
comes toward me with a machete
ready to defend her thatch hut,
sheep, balding chickens.
She understands only Quechuan,
grimace and gesture.
She lets me pass.

Overnight beside the snow line,
my canteen freezes to brick.
Before dawn, I chip ice
with a pickaxe, suck,
work gloved hands
into strongholds
to hoist myself up
jagged rock.

From the peak
a tumult of summits glimmer,
then douse in blur and mist.
A cloud envelopes the range.
I struggle to breathe.

Finally mist clears.
On a lake below,
infinitesimal men
in an infinitesimal boat cast nets.
Tatters of their cries rise.

Wind whips my jacket.
I descend having been warned
in no uncertain terms
that avalanches begin
as soon as the sun gains power.

BLANKETS

Huancayo, Peru   March 2019

Mountain passes exhale frigid wind.
Andean nights are dank and penetrating.

The blankets locals use are heavy mated affairs –
alpaca fiber tightly woven. Wool's weight works
the way a cat in a lap relaxes muscle down to the bone,

ribs, shoulders, elbows, hips, knees, ankles.
Blankets soften the sleeper's profile.

Most nights in Peru I lay still
as a petroglyph sunken in a cave.

THE PAST IS THE FUTURE

Huancayo, Peru   June 1979

In Concepcion where the Church of the Blessed Virgin
rings its bells, men carve, pound, shape
silver jewelry of delectable intricacy.

Beside their sheep, chickens, alpaca, cattle,
Quechuan women in the Huayhuash range
weave alpaca wool the way they have
since before the Spaniards came.

In Cochas Chico men etch stories,
landscapes, patterns into gourds.
They roll the embers of smoking ash wood
across the gourd to sear in shade and depth,
tell, retell the stories of their lives.

Men plow. Women wash.
In the shadows of these mountains
boys become who their father is,
girls become who their mother is.

TALONS

Cochas Chico, Peru   September 2017

In the middle of the night
on a twenty-two hour bus ride
from Quito to Lima, all the passengers
are jolted awake, prodded across a parking lot
filled with exhaust fumes from squads of idling buses.

We file into a blare of restaurant light,
sit down at a table with utensils and a bowl of chicken soup
that has two chicken talons, resting in broth.

That is how it is served here,
broth, carrot, celery, onion, talons.
Over the months I begin to suck sweet, fatty skin
off the bone clean as any local.

I learn to get up a mountainside by chewing coca.
I learn to perch on cement starter blocks.
crap into a hole. I swill *Aguardiente.*

In Cochas my host serves me *pachamanca* –
meat and corn slow-cooked, smoldered
overnight on coals covered with dirt.

By the time I get back home
nothing will stop me.

ON THE ALTIPLANO

Peru   June 1979

In Ayacucho and Huancayo women sit
in shade on chair seats of woven rush,
drink beer under broad-brim hats.

Women walk the *calles*
with loaded, bulging blankets
slung across their backs.
Work, grin, and jabber
under hats that tell what
place they come from.

Understand – time in mountains
is different from time by the sea.

Hats are passed on down from grandmothers.
The women of Huancayo and Ayacucho
have tanned, sun-stroked skin.
The earth swells and comes alive
in their chests, hands, and laps.

Boulder, brook, eucalyptus, star,
patience, seed, clod, condor
all pass under the brims of these
good women's weathered hats.

THE WHITE CITY OF ETERNAL SPRING

Arequipa, Peru   May 1979

Beneath the skirt of a volcanic cone,
trade winds sweep in from the Pacific,
over streets warm as baked cookies.

Arequipa's architecture is grand and Spanish
with walls made from an alabaster pumice.
Great chunks of white stone snuggle.
One stone atop another, walls shimmer.

Bougainvillea spills over gateways.
Doves, parrots whip in and out of palms.
The scent of eucalyptus fills the afternoons.

Raised Catholic, bedeviled by guilt,
I fly out the second day suspecting
that I will never be able to purify myself
enough to deserve such beauty.

CONDOR

Ollantaytambo, Peru   July 1979

When I was young and wild to get everywhere
I hiked ranges where planes get struck by lightning,
pirouette and disappear in the Eastern Cordelia
where vines and brush engulf anything within three years.
That's how the Inca went lost for centuries.

I can sometimes calm my pulse
by remembering an afternoon
when I hiked on a ridge above
a river that crashed and threaded
its way toward Machu Picchu.

A condor passed close enough
for me to hear the whistle off its wing.
And, so, I will not die without knowing glory
amidst the ceaseless struggles
of stone and wind.

SOME THINGS CHANGE, SOME DO NOT

Huancayo, Peru   March 2019

In 1979, Huancayo was a dot on the map —
six bus routes, one hotel. Forty years have passed.

On the bus ride to Cochas I'd often spy a man
who stood on a wooden plow dragged by an ox.
Now teens with book sacks scurry
at a high school where he rode
over the rocky sea of his rows.

In the interim there was a revolution.
The Shining Path took over the city.
Bombs blew limbs through storefronts,
carved bodies into Cubist portraits.

Now there are pharmacies, supermarkets,
beauty parlors everywhere. So much honking,
taxis, bustle. I feel misplaced.

Women still go to and from the market
with goods wrapped in colorful blankets
lashed across their backs.
Small boys now have shoes.

Salcantay Trail

Salcantay Trail, Peru   April 2019

As soon as we hear hoof-strikes around blind corners,
we sidestep, plaster ourselves against cliff walls
where mineral water drips through moss.

A line of packhorses rumbles by
roped down with brilliant blankets,
sacks, pots that clack and quake
as they clop toward the next camp.

We step back to a path lined with trumpet flowers,
bells, stars, slippers – flowers that cover stamen
under hoods, heavily pollinated buds
where bees disappear into urns formed
out of petals. Orchids dip over our shoulders.

For two days we slog over muck, rock, scree,
trickles – silver on silver, silver on black –
and over road apples covered in butterflies.
In intoxicated loops, orchestral flurries,
butterflies rise and bat against our hands and cheeks,
then settle back onto mounds in the path.

Because, after all, they are just angel-winged flies
and the road to heaven is never how you think.

COFFEE GOOD FRIDAY MORNING

Salcantay Trail, Peru   April 2019

I sip coffee from beans plucked out of shade
on the side of an Andean mountain
by me, my daughter, and my son-in-law.
We were shown how to whisk the beans
over a splay of fire, a few lit twigs.

With quick wrists we stirred beans in a clay pot.
"Mas rapido, mas rapido" the bean farmer urged
until the beans gained the dark aroma
I now enjoy back in Louisiana

where green leaves wag in spring wind.
Robust branches are what my eyes see
as this rich brew takes me back

onto that mountainside where every muscle ached
after a three-day hike over wind-punished passes,
along ledges, under snow caps. Then down
into mists, dangled orchids, flocks of butterflies
as we picked out steps through roots and muck.

At that coffee farm I could have clicked a photo
of my daughter when she lifted a long bamboo pole
to work the edge of a tiny net tied onto the pole's tip
against an avocado stem. There, avocado trees
grow to thirty feet. The avocado gave way, dropped
into the net. She brought it down. Handed the fruit
to a women dressed in heavy mountain garb
who placed the avocado on a ledge in sunlight.

I could have taken that photo but I was too ragged,
too exhausted, too at peace with everything I had
ever done and could not move one single muscle
except to watch two eagles lift into great helixes
of wind that disappeared behind tail feathers.

THE INCA'S SACRED MOUNTAIN

Humantay Pass, Peru   April 2019

If an old man can still
inch himself up Salcantay,
boot over stone,
gasp for breath,

can pass below
peak's glacial ice,
brace bones against gusts,

camp as the southern cross,
night's wide carriage,
rolls its monstrous wheel,

won't he be altered,
alchemized,

to stand again
          ancient
among ancients.

THE CONTIGUOUS

PERDITION

Route 66, Oklahoma, Texas, New Mexico   June 1969

I manage to hitch a ride
with a Brother in a Caddy.
He dials up Funk and Motown
all the way from Tulsa to Albuquerque.

That Caddy sails through the red dirt gulches
of Oklahoma and then across the Texas panhandle,
which is like having to pass through purgatory
before being trap-doored down into brimstone.

In the panhandle some lone-star, hometown hero
pulls us over on account of seeing a skinny white boy
in a fine machine with a well-dressed son of Kenya
is way too much for his belief system.

Not that it surprises me
to find racists in Texas
but who ever thought hell had cops.

LANGTRY, LOADED WITH SKY.

Langtry, Texas   April 2017

Del Rio to Marathon, 178 miles of lizard belly,
lizard belly and gulches that swallow the sun.
Halfway there is the Judge Roy Bean Museum,
where some of this state's legends of cruelty
are enshrined in a one-block town.
On Highway 90 I find a quick-stop
beside a three-room motel with sand
blown in by each doorstep. No sign, so
I call it "House of Dismal Encounters."

The station has one gas pump
which is rusted, dusty and dry, gulch dry.
When I go in, the donut-eater/clerk
croaks out that a Texaco tanker
might roll in by Thursday.
Then again, could be Saturday.

She holds a finger up, saunters off.
Reemerges with a wickedly long-tailed funnel
and a two-gallon gas can red as turkey wattle.
She offers me the contents for twelve dollars
which is way cheaper than three nights abed
between the Motel Dismal's scratchy sheets.

So I watch the quick-stop turn
to a sand grain in the rearview.
Tires spin on over asphalt, state-maintained
to insure ease of access for Texans' and tourists'
journeys through hell's wide landscape.

A Pocked and Banded Stone

Outside Del City, Texas   March 1973

I sleep three nights in the desert a dozen miles
north of the Rio Grande. I count thirty-four
night-crossers that stumble over terrain designed for reptiles.
In a cattle pen, I lean against splintery fencing
to eat lunch with a man from Zacatecas.

The man unrolls tortillas from a bandana.
I share my Van Camp's beans.
He is headed toward Aurora, Illinois
where his brother winds copper
for appliance motors eight hours a day.
The man stammers out the inflected question,
 "Momma?" – hangs on every word of my slow reply.

I do not tell him I am in the desert
to leave my mother and every single thing
that has formed me behind.
That I grew up and left a place
one county away from where he is headed.
We both know that a desert erases the past.

Later that afternoon I come across a rare stone
that is blanched white, pocked as if fallen from the moon
with prismatic arcs across it, soft pastel bands.

I try to mark the spot, come back later
but cannot find it again. The next morning
I walk out ten miles east, then seven more north.
I hitch to Louisiana which is green.
Forty years later, I am still in lush Louisiana.

Sometimes I imagine that rock
is a timeless egg that the shadow
of a pterodactyl still passes across.

I do not need to go back.
I know that stone will survive anything,
will stay lodged under the blare of the sun
indelible and isolate as the soul.

SKUNKED ANGELS

Sabine Pass, Texas   August 1977

My fellow deckhand, Ronnie,
escaped a gang of Nashville dealers,
hitched down to the Gulf
to cold turkey off heroin.
I'm just tying bowlines for summer bucks.
On a deadbeat Saturday, Ronnie
hooks us up with a local yahoo
stoned out of his gourd by 4 p.m.

We loll on this home-boy's front porch.
He doesn't move or twitch for a half hour.
Then two hummingbirds dip and join
at the hip just above tridents of canna lilies.
The guy throws his head back and cries out,
"Damn if that ain't cuter than a spotted pup
in a new red wagon."

The three of us end up at last call
in a bar with an interior decor
like an oil slick on wrenched seas.
Everyone is stiff, silent, pickled
until the needle drops
into K23 on the jukebox.

Deckhands, crew-boat captains, Ronnie,
home-boy, boiler masters and a few Debs,
start to sing in unison to no one in particular –
low, breathy bent into bar or table tops
where brown bottles are microphones.
It's a chorus of skunked angels,
without a soprano in the bunch.
("Back in Luckenbach, Texas,
ain't nobody feeling no pain.")
We sing as if these words
hold the only hope around
and the song itself is what
sheds light off mirror glass.

DUST AND HALLUCINATION

Orange, Texas   March 1973

I hitch east from El Paso through terrain
so void I could be on an asteroid.
In the diners Texans have hidden
cockroach eyes, skin so dry they crackle.
The point of West Texas
is to get out of West Texas.

I ride shotgun, watch a hawk
circle painfully slow. Time flat melts
inside that carrion's widening gyre
like boredom is an acid I've dropped
and nothing, not a thing, can ever be redeemed.

The second day I make Orange, Texas.
Orange is a post-apocalyptic, industrial nightmare
interrupted by towering stratocumulus of oak.
In order to make it beyond the interminable
yawn of Texas without clawing my eyes out,
I pretend I am earning time off of Purgatory.
I offer my eyes up to the sky.

LATE NIGHT

Vernon, Texas   March 2013

Often, I end up in a nondescript motel
needing something. I find a quick-stop
where grime multiplies under pale fluorescence.
The squared-off fingers of a store owner
punch the register. Large knuckles
mean the man or woman is stubborn,
determined, analytical, which all bode well
for running a business. These owners

mop their own linoleum, hawk-eye
riff-raff that try to palm candy bars,
slide Buds into hoodie pockets
or pop a Glock out of jeans.

They comb customers over,
calculate risks. Under their eyes,
I begin to catalogue
my own character flaws, the ones
I've known since second grade
when Sister Mary Cristobal
first started the list.

THE SUNSET STRIP ET AL

California   June 1969

I

Tell mom and dad that I am fine, though "fine"
is relative. An off-duty cop dropped me
onto Sunset Strip concrete last night
with warnings to be careful.
I slept on a mattress at the back of an alleyway
blocked from the street by a cedar fence.

Before eight a.m., I got an invite for coffee at Vips –
"Home of the Big Boy" – from a man in a suit
who sipped, took his time while he let
what he really wanted slowly dawn on me.

I must look green, lost amid these tattered jeans,
miniskirts, palm fronds, Jaguars, do-rags,
acid tabs, Jesus Freaks, bikers, bus exhaust,
Hare Krishnas, "Hare-Hare" and Ganja.

I've hitchhiked a thousand miles
to escape the tedium of cornfields.
Everybody's got a hustle. Traffic, horns.
Grime on sidewalks. The smell of fresh piss.

II

Trying to hitch to San Francisco
I got picked up by a long hair
who swung me by his house in the valley.

There a girl called Alice, all of fifteen,
wore a peasant skirt, granny glasses,
set two cups and a teapot beside her mattress
on the floor in a house where the couple raises chickens,
goats and children down a dead-end gravel road. Everyone
there drops acid on Sundays.
To earn her keep, Alice collects eggs,
sweeps, scours, baby-sits, bakes.

Have you ever seen anyone shrink as their voice
grows softer and softer until they seem a small doll?
Alice seemed to get so shrunken, I could have shaken
what little I have out of my bag, stuffed her in
beside the bedroll, snuck her out.
We could have hitchhiked together into a fairy tale
I would have written as we went along.

ABOVE THE DROWNED CAVES

Hoover Dam, Nevada   June 2013

We came upon Hoover Dam on U.S. 93
without knowing it would be there.
Out of drought, back into drought —
a structure built to break the will of drought.

The dam's concrete smooth, bowed,
strong enough to restrain the Colorado,
transform cascades and steely currents
into one-hundred-twenty miles of lake.

Living within this chiseled chasm,
ancients once worked out a way
to sustain themselves beside
sidewinder, vulture, jackrabbit.
Ancients walked, climbed, slept, ate
in the pockets of cliff caves,
left mostly shards, arrow and axe heads.

Their scant, submerged petrography
records how they venerated a desert's meager gifts
as sun scorched their skin, as sun stained
strata upon strata, upon strata
with bands of tangerine, rose, sulfur, lilac.

I believe those ancients venerated
a river that still gives sustenance,
venerated land as dynamite, concrete
and bulldozers never do.

JUST SAYING

Sitka, Kansas   May 2016

It takes time to get across Kansas.
Tumbleweed blows from Oklahoma to Nebraska
and back without much trouble except when it
pinballs through a herd of sleeping cows.

I'd have stayed too,
if I'd broken both legs and an arm.
Before telephones and TVs
a lot of Kansans shot each other
just for a break in routine.

In land empty as a mirror,
you have time to think. I thought,
Why did Dorothy even want to go back?
She was already a freakin' orphan.
She'd made friends. Even if the wizard was fizz,
Glinda could solve stuff. Plus,
Oz had singing wee folk
that laced adorable feet into doll shoes.

FRAME

Arches National Park, Utah   May 2016

Sandstone arches,
scrimshawed by wind
have endured tectonic shifts,
blizzards, blistering heat
to frame tumults of rock.

Rust, rose, violet and lemon strata
mark eons from long before
Europeans arrived with pick axes,
dynamite, backhoes – times before
any paw, horse hoof or wheel
moved across winter under starlight.

The arches frame flowing currents
in stone that mingle, waver and swell
in aggregate the way voices, breath
and sea tides pitch, shift
 and falter, but slower.

EARS OF THE DEAD

Taos, New Mexico   August 2016

On the rarified sierra, mustangs thunder.
Near town, magpies drag tail feathers,
skirt and flit. We find an adobe hotel,
leave the door ajar. Mountains dust up purple.

Come sunup, we are at the famous pueblo.
When I try to photograph a sequestered cemetery,
a guard shouts me away. Maybe he believes
cell phones capture dead souls.

We stop under willow by a brook.
There I try on the ears of the dead
to hear every vowel, every whisper
of turbulence, loss and joy that brook
has ever known and can pronounce.

WHIPPOORWILL

Eureka Springs, Arkansas   June 1982

Give me the rustle of a dry field,
wood posts tilted akilter
as if bobbing upon a great sea

because that is how these hills and hollers
surge and dip in their vast tide of stone.

Throw in a blaze of tangerine
as sun slides below the horizon.
Add the three plaintive notes
of a whippoorwill. Three
plaintive notes that come,
come again, come thrice
in thin wind.

Let me lag in the silence
between this bird's gentle sobs.
You can have the rest.

IN THE GREEN MOUNTAINS

Ripton, Vermont   June 1972

I

It took me two hours
up a pitch path,
over root and rock,
to discover that
next to dawn everything
I've ever known is useless.

Ridge upon ridge
set even as ribs
rise and fall, fall and rise
as the sun breathes
over crests. Fog flows
through valleys.

Fragile as moth wings,
words fall apart
before this nodding sea
of time, mist, stone.

II

I sleep on the ground in a tent
along the Green Mountain Trail
near a lake of shimmer and perch
and discover that leeches
can't set their hooks into skin
if I wriggle, twist, never cease.

Pools of blueberry bushes
swell along mountain paths.
Stars here are different
from the lackluster things
we gaped at in Illinois.
Galaxies lean in.

Yesterday we leapt off a ledge
into a cold brook that pooled
to fifteen feet deep
at the bottom of a waterfall,
came up dripping diamonds.
Mornings and evenings are so quiet,
I could be a letter in a sealed envelope.
If I didn't have to make a living,
I would only leave at gunpoint.

AFTER LITERARY HIGH-TIMES AT BREAD LOAF

Baltimore, Maryland   August 1972

I end up at my sister's trying to decide what to do.
Shouldn't I go back to Racine, sign on
for another season of dismal
punching sheet metal in a factory,
where the final whistle blows us out to the bar
to perform ablutions of the throat and heart
with deep drafts, cold washes of beer?
Isn't that how I can learn to love Teri
enough not to wander again?

At the National Gallery in Washington
a guard follows me room to room
as if I have criminal intent
until they dim the lights,
usher the public out for the night.

I ride a commuter back to Baltimore.
On the way to my sister's apartment,
the sun sets, cayenne crisscrossed by chain-link
down an alleyway of shattered glass,
fire escapes, steel doors,
a mattress tilted up in a dumpster.

I stand transfixed
as if this scene is a penance,
a karma I have been assigned.
From a landing, a German Shepherd barks.

Concrete and brick darken. Cones
of street lamp almost touch. I walk on,
inhale the incense of night.

PANTHER CREEK

Panther Creek, Georgia   November 2002

I

Some days are mist and rain.
Some days I sprawl on outcroppings
where flies and bees orbit
mad to be close to the sun.

There is more decay and rot in these forests,
time-softened ridges than one would guess.
White-tail does whisk off. I munch trail-mix
under a pine trunk with a wicked scar
where lightning striped its bark.

The backpack bites into my shoulders.
I sweat bullets. No one else for miles.
Thrush, bunting, red beetle,
stripes down the chipmunk's back.

Muscles groan, tighten. Sometimes
cataracts fall, ice-white. In any going on,
there is some small bravery.
If the mountain continues to mountain
shouldn't someone bear witness?
At night constellations come close.

II

I go as far away as a body can, hike
to where stone speaks with stone's tongue.
The silver trills of this shot-cold brook,
its surge and whirl, comb and tumble,
comes gratis beneath stars.

I sleep in a sleeping bag by the bank,
which seems, to me, a primo way to dream
if you are not afraid to put eternity
in a cup and drink.

I Go Back

Warrenville, Illinois   February 2006

I am here for the Bears-Saints playoff game,
but that doesn't matter. Instead
what I want you to know is that
one can travel too much.

A full moon mesmerizes anywhere:
draped over moss along a bayou,

through splashes of shade
that wag along an Appalachian path,

on the faces of churchyard tombstones,
or yanked apart, put back together in pond water.

Tonight we have a new moon, slender
not long after sunset over Warrenville, IL

the town where I began, the town where our parents,
my brother, two grandparents lie under granite.

What matters is how against great odds,
the moon can slip out from behind

years of clouds to stamp
its own brand of hope.

THE MONKEY

Chicago, Illinois   July 2011

Renee was determined to meet my family.
Three hours out from the flight something
terribly strange appeared in her left eye –
a black gap – a cavern edged
with an aurora borealis of charged particles.
She insisted we board the flight.

At our reunion picnic Renee slathered butter
over corn on the cob. We walked by Chi-town's
oceanic lake. Her figure bloated and slimmed
in the funny-mirror chrome of "The Bean."
She inhaled cigar smoke, notes of Bud,
hot dog steam at Wrigley Field.
She straddled the knee of one of the great,
stone lions on the Art Institute's steps.

At least she saw a good fraction of that,
walked through the long weekend
without giving an inkling
that she was suddenly half-blind

and had the monkey
of impending eye surgery
on her back.

WOE BABY

Menominee Falls, Wisconsin   April 2013

You have to develop a knack for passing
under the archway of sleep in strange places.

In Athens we took to the couches,
threw open windows. The clatter,
grind, hiss and roar of traffic
pored its oceanic wash into our ears.

At the snow line in Peru,
I had to put on two tee shirts
and three pairs of socks,
shiver off in my sleep sack.

On a ridge near Albuquerque
I listened to coyote howl
and pretended clouds that drifted
under the moon were a great armada
nodding their way across the Milky Way.

But in this Milwaukee suburb, whoa baby,
anyone can nod off mid-sentence.

Gossamer

New York, New York   October 1984

I fly into Gotham around six
but my host, Jack, is out of town till ten.

No problem, the New Yorker says
Joe Pass will be at Smalls Jazz Club on West 10th.
Catch a cab. First show at nine.

Straight away, I order a single-malt scotch
that has curls of smoke livened up
with two dashes of sea salt
just to let city folk know
Southerners can be pretentious too.

Turns out the bartender, Alex, went to LSU.
Alex slides me free Macallans, neat,
icewater on the side. Alex jots down
the number of an aspiring
goddess/actress we both know
who just moved back from LA to the suddenly
warm, ripe, juicy, intimate Big Apple.

The third scotch is always a strike.
By nine thirty I am a fly
wrapped in the gossamer threads
that Joe Pass' fingers weave fret by fret,
ten digits each quick as a spider's foot
as silk sails out of the belly of his guitar.

CAROLINA

Chapel Hill, North Carolina   September 2019

Red leaf imbedded in dank dirt.
Muck on a flattened gum wrapper.
Buttery bib of a warbler on ash branch.

Branches, twigs down, feed fungus,
ants, algae, fleck back to soil.

Where our path meets the creek
current shoots left, fans wide.
The serpent works ribs against earth.

Chrome and black creek water
billows before it tumbles under tree roots,
unties its own knot, slithers on
dead-black and silver, braided.

Reeds across the way translucent,
in what light slants this low.
Splash of ferns behind.

A fly lands. I flick it. Wind and lemon
rush through high canopy, rattle.

Later we sit on our friend's patio.
Quiet talk between sips.
She has tea, he beer. Renee—white wine.
Scotch in my paw. Trees tick in mist.

Not far off an ambulance whines
up a mountain road, the fact made
plain how effortless it will be
for this to go on without
any one of us.

WHAT LARKS

Grand Isle, Louisiana   March 2019

Every March, faithful as the birds
that beat their wings across desolate waves
all the way from the Yucatan
to finally catch a breath on this shore,
Renee and I drive down for the Grand Isle
Ancient Athletes Basketball Tournament.

In the hollows of camellia bushes
indigo buntings pant. Robins, thrush
cling to zig-zag twigs up
and down this barrier island.

With old friends, we feast on crawfish,
uncork Pinot, Chardonnay, stay up
into the wee, pantomime tales,
doubleover with glee. In dozens
of glorious, dubious ways we act
in the manner that every parent
cautions their children to never adopt.

One weekend a year our small cadre
strikes careless postures in beach chairs
as heart conditions, divorce and arthritis
advance their causes and the occasional
hurricane dismantles houses, tosses small birds.

A SLOW CUP, SAVORED

St. Petersburg, Florida   November 2015

Back when, I couldn't slow down,
not enough. Coffee is a good teacher.

All these waiters' sneakers pip and squeal
intermittent as freshly hatched penguins.
Brakes of a city bus, its rev,
then the vacuum left in its wake.
Newspaper flipped, folded.
Three page corners flap
in the mercy of a Gulf breeze.

The complicated geometry of a spider web
spun through the wrought iron legs
of a bistro table. Curls
in a dried leaf caught there.

A jogger in Nikes flies by
quicker than cabbies can.
When I lift my cup, clouds
appear in the coffee's mirror.
A man with a Pomeranian on a leash
spills nibbles. The light changes.

I smell a nasty squall as it trundles in
from off the coast of the Yucatan.

BAY OF FUNDY

St Clair Point, Nova Scotia   July 2004

I

Coast tattered under fog,
sea-lapped stone, seal yelps.
Mists and tide wash calendars,
appointments, idle plans away.

What is left is the next meal.
Maybe scallops netted
as they drift among plankton,
clams clawed out of sand
or lobster, cage-caught,
submerged in sea swell.

At night a ceaseless, shrill wind
carries out the moans of widows, mothers;
carries in the cries of men and boys
lost beyond the turmoil of the breakers.
Only the bones of loneliness here.

II

We ripped across the Bay of Fundy
at fifty knots on a state-of-the-art car ferry
replete with a martini bar and slots.
We have two and a half days
before I fly back to Louisiana.
The Nissan will stay eight weeks
with Louise and the children
for the drive home after she finishes
French immersion courses
on the fog draped, wind plied
shores of Nova Scotia
where whales sound, blow fume.
Seal bob amid swirls of seaweed, brine.
I kick up flotsam stuck into sand
and watch my daughters
dart after ghost-white crabs.

Louise has barely spoken
since we left Atlanta.
She has chosen this trip
to an island immersed
in mist and isolation
as a way to make sure
that I understand
our marriage is over.

THE BIG EASY

New Orleans, Louisiana   March 2017

There are so many streets, hours, faces
in New Orleans that you turn upon, walk toward
like you are stepping into a painting.

Maybe you are in the artist's studio.
Jazz pours out of speakers
in a lazy, post-coital river.

The painting needs only
a few more strokes. A shaded
swatch of jade, a blood-orange streak
where sunset finds the horizon, topaz
soft as bottle glass washed in the sea.

The painting needs just
a half glass more of wine.

Decade after decade people jet in.
From all over the world,
they punch their tickets for beauty.

TWO DAYS AFTER PAPERS FOR LEGAL SEPARATION ARE FILED

Sikeston, Missouri   January 2002

Motel curtains hold the memory
of Marlboros, Virginia Slims,
Kent Menthols. My daughters
are being tucked in without me.

There is a truck stop
a third of a mile down,
ice in strips, street lamps.
The interstate thunders
under eighteen-wheelers.

Pebbles, broken glass and cinder
lie in lines beside asphalt.
Next to that: weeds, fence
and a field—snow-patched,

abandoned. I stand a long time,
frozen, maybe cryogenic,
at the lip of an invisible chasm,
a vast rift in the night.
I try to reconfigure a history
I will never make it back into.

ON VACA

Shreveport, Louisiana   May 2015

We drove out under a deluge
that will later make national news.
Hundreds of Baton Rouge houses
flooded up to the fuse box.

The visibility was nil.
Just shy of I-20 rain finally pulled off
but the Kia's engine started to miss.
An Autozone clerk tattooed
in scenes from Thermopylae
had a hand-held analyzer
that told him the what's-it was shot.

He dialed a mechanic, who pulled in,
fixed the Kia on the spot—one-fifty flat, cash—
while we watched a girl get cuffed,
laid down on the strip mall sidewalk.
Cops ripped a baggie out from her jeans,
held it up, nodded. Meth, Coke, Oxi—I couldn't tell.

Sometimes you head somewhere
but you get somewhere else.

A SMALL, GOOD PLACE

Mentone, Alabama April 2021

I

Ridges nudge one another soft
as loaves on a baker's rack. Appalachian soils
are molded like blankets over the hips,
ribs, shoulders of an old man
that tosses between sleep and death.

Constellations diamond above wind-turned leaves.
Eons-old light has crossed galaxies, frigid
rivers of wind to prick into this pocket
of night that so few know.

Here the Appalachian chain buckles
at its Southern terminus, tucks itself to rest.
Renee and I have driven hundreds of miles
to sit beside a fire with friends
in this living archeological site
that history never even got to.

We sit, sip, talk, look up
at shards of light.

II

You might angle your boot out
to a small rhomboid of earth framed by rock,
then launch up a boulder, gambol
across the crowns of five more stones.

You learn how to loosen joints, become a Nureyev
among stone fall, a Fred Astaire
whose steps patter over a cascade of cobble.

One minute a trek has the rhythm of roofers
at blows with broad nail heads.
Next you plod your donkey-hooves
along a loopy ridge.

Then again, nimble as a brook trout,
feet swish between curled roots,
lift across the spines of nested stones.
In my ears the whole morning, thunder
as arpeggios of river-fall shatter on rock.

THE BEEHIVE

Mount Desert Island, Maine   September 2021

We clamber over boulders,
rockface scored by glaciers,
gripped by spruce and maple root.
We pass scrub, frothed Moose-Moss,
fallen trunks covered with Witch's Butter.

Orange, grey and dun mushroom caps,
lichen — clean scents of things that stay,
that have propagated themselves for eons,
multiply under rain, snow, broken sunlight.

Brooks cascade, shatter on, slice into stone,
then disappear shaded, tumultuous.

Finally, we stand at the summit.
Below, the Atlantic shows seven shades
ablaze in blue: jay's wing feathers the bay,
a sapphire shimmers where mackerel boats bob,
drop nets into a current between shore
and the westernmost Cranberry Island
— flecks of mica on those wave backs.

Gunmetal blue as tide
pulls its string on nine coves.
Where waves smite rock
marine and mercury saw.

Swells rise into pools of turquoise
through which jade glows. A scarf
of cobalt wavers beyond the islands.
In the distance a ghosted fog blankets
a shade pale, trembling, glacial.

Oh mother of blues, boundless bounty,
joy shivers my bones on top of stone.

WE BECOME A PAIR OF CROWS IN THE ROCKIES

Estes Park, Colorado   October 2021

We have not yet trekked over treacherous ice
by mountain lakes, whey-blue and filled
with pike, perch that glide along the shore.

All we know yet is the imposing glory
of glacial peaks that lift in a ring, peaks
it takes the sun hours to climb over,
seconds to slip behind and leave
moonlight to bone cold stone.

In the parking lot of a strip mall
we discuss what pleasure we could have
if we buy two plastic Adirondack chairs
from the True Value store
and sit beside our rented Buick
to snack, read, chat and gawk.

IN A PICKUP BED

MOTHER MARY, WHO LISTENS, ALWAYS

Juarez, Mexico   January, 1973

A stone white cathedral stands beside the plaza
Along its walls glass encased tableaus
show martyrs with stab-wounds,
a nailed Christ in his halo of thorns.

Off the sanctuary I find a wooden Mary.
Her robes hang brown as bark.
Her shoulder wrap is the turquoise
of glacial pools under peaks. Golden threads
stitch the hems of Mary's garments.

The man who painstakingly carved,
then painted this Mary took the time,
as he ached for succor, to form

Mary's ears into miracles,
whirlpools into which
any sinner or seeker
can pour their troubled days.

GOOD CONCH

San Pedro Island, Belize   April 1990

The sun is a beast above palms.
Mercury soars. If we sit in shade,
we stay fresh as martinis.

Ceaseless wind combs the beach.
If we step out of shade and are behind
a building that blocks wind, we stagger
in a blast of furnace heat.

Then we have to force our steps
until we get beyond the building's walls.
Trade winds pick back up,
lift and ply our feathers.
Is there a harp nearby?
Aren't we, again, fresh gin?

Last night star-points shook through palm fronds
as we worked our toes into sand, tasted
good conch heated in a bed of coals,
smothered in butter.

Rows of Eel's Teeth

San Pedro Island, Belize   April 1990

I

The small craft has a coke-bottle bottom.
Veined fans of coral nod, translucent
in the sea-saw wash. Sea horses, tang fish
slip sideways through keyhole gaps in coral.

We gear up – snorkel, mask and fins,
drop into waves, bob. Our guide yells,
"Follow me. A moray eel has a cave here."
I follow. Without warning, the guide
flings food, pedals backwards.
A seven-foot eel shoots up
in front of my mask, gobbles chum.

Meanwhile the captain has to leave
our anchored craft, dive in to save poor Louise
who, on our honeymoon, has been left behind
to gasp, slap, pop up and down on swells and waves.

Unbeknownst, one-hundred feet behind me,
my new bride is rescued by the boat captain.
I snorkel among clown and zebra fish,
awake in a place of dreaming.

II

Louise lathers limbs and torso, soaks in sun, or reads
under the ceiling fan in our cabin, seldom swims.
During the wedding her face turned sallow and green.

She doesn't say much. Under water veined, violet fans
of coral undulate semi-substantial as a summer dress,
sway to the rhythm of Caribbean waves.
My snorkel mask comes face to face
with two immaculate rows of eel's teeth
as the beast snaps up chum the guide flung out.

Night stars are fat. Louise is asleep
by the time I come in from walks.

Our first day on the island,
I sliced my foot on bottle glass.
Now the wound is angry,
throbs red. I soak toilet paper
in rum, treat the wound
the same way I treat any trouble.

PURPLE BLOOMS

San Miguel de Allende, Mexico   May, 2007

I

I count the rings, from nine tolling towers,
most faint, two an easy stroll away.

Tuesday and Friday afternoons,
an apprentice walks beside a van
that rolls forward at the pace of the apprentice
as he bangs a file against a machete,
makes them chime.

The man that pushes a fruit cart up the street
jets out one sharp, two longer whistles.
The garbage truck lays into the horn
every other block. These announcements

roll their slow parades, give folks time
to fly down staircases, flag them at the curb
where a river of people ripple by
in clothes as varied as summer flowers
day and night, night and day,
half of their faces carved from stone.

II

At a cactus stubbled park, bees, birds, dragonflies
vibrate, shoot, flit bloom-to-branch-to-bloom.
A cataract cuts veins and chasms through
Tawny, ore-red, ocher soil. Streams crash
toward a distant lake the color of flu.

We find a pavilion. As the sun pales beyond sand-motes,
Juan uses a bench for a drum. I breathe into the flute.

Heading out, Juan pockets two-dozen paddle cactus blooms.
Less than two hours later Juan uses those buds
to whip up a savory, purple sauce.

We down Merlot, gab, eat on a table top
made out of a door and set up on the roof
under the gleaming teeth of Mexican stars.

GOLD, RED, VIOLET, MAGENTA

San Miguel de Allende, Mexico   June, 2005

We are in a city of church domes
rimmed round by mountains
that twice a parched day
swirl purpled dust motes
over the face of far-off peaks.
Fireworks crowd night skies.

Our apartment lets out onto a tiled roof
of pigeons, clutter and clatter.
Dawn and dusk, dusk and dawn,
church bells clang. Before we wake,

sometimes before we finally get to bed,
a rooster perched above a water heater
cries out to the sun as if the sun
is a twin that wandered from its home.

The rooster screams
with raw, jagged passion,
tries to wretch his balls up
through his red and golden throat.

INSIDE

San Miguel de Allende, Mexico   May 2007

Beneath domes of inlaid cobalt tiles
that each opened to a cup of sky,
you and your daughter giggled, swam.

Three successive bath chambers, each mineral,
each rimmed round under domes,
each more steamy than the last.
Water bone-softening as soup.

You did not come to me then
the way you come to me now.

You cradled your daughter's neck and head
so she could float arrow-straight, feet up.
Your eyes welled jewel bright
above the rills of sapphire pools.

I did not know yet
how I would come to seek
my own sky inside those eyes.

IN A PICKUP BED

Guanajuato, Mexico   May 2008

From pumps a shave off the highway,
Juan funnels gas. Curs sleep in the heat.
The store front seems flat, the way
western sets prop on two-by-fours.

You and I jostle in the back bed.
Up in the cab, Juan and Meagan
laugh, reel, pause, then roar again.
These are your grown children.
I am getting to know them.
Hell, I'm still getting to know you.

We cross a plateau cut by gullies.
Buzzards hop sideways, then
back in to hunker over road kill.
Our destination is an old mining town
with cobbled streets, a masonry mission,
sun-blanched tower that hoists a bell.

At a restaurant, the owner's wife
is the server. Her voice is full, melodic.
The tortilla soup is good.

On the way home rain starts to splat.
Juan finds two polyurethane bags.
I rip out arm and head holes.
Your hair plasters to your forehead, cheeks.
We lose our voices in the rain.

That is when I realize
we can withstand anything,
that it is stupid to ever want
one single thing other than what we have.

GARGOYLES, EMPIRES, A SHOELACE

LUMPY

Paris, France   June 1991

We have an address.
If you've never driven in Paris,
you've never known misery.

Out of respect for history,
one-way streets change names,
about-face 180 degrees without warning.
You have to decide – turn left, turn right?
Cars behind lean on their horns.

We end up at the same traffic circle four times.
We break for lunch, mine, a sublime crepe.
The map is useless. The map is a maze.
We are the rats. Everything is older
than you can imagine. Streets whip around,
cross over as convoluted as spaghetti noodles.

The day blares on. Even the lumpiest
hotel mattress can be a gift from God.

SHOELACE

Paris, France   June 1991

In the basement of the Louvre,
Miriam's tiny finger pointed
at the sculpture of a man
with the head of a falcon,
another with the lithe,
muscled body of a lion.

On a morning when a fan
who stood in a crowd behind ropes
was struck by lightning at the eleventh green
during the U.S. Open in Chaska, Minnesota,
Miriam and I were often the only two
in the basement of the Louvre.

She was awed. I was awed.
Our mouths dropped agape.
No doubt the troops were awed
as Napoleon plundered Egypt
for the glory that is France.

As we made our way back up,
Miriam's shoelace caught
in the escalator's jaws.
I felt a sudden tug. Instinctively
I ripped her up into my arms.

That engine could have
shredded her foot
with only a shudder.

We stood to the side.
Crowds filed by blank-faced,
as if fate and history
can be held at arm's length,
are things printed in guidebooks.

IN THE SACRISTY

Paris, France   June 1991

At Notre Dame I point out archways,
gargoyle mouths agape
to splatter sidewalks with spilled rain.

I carry my daughter
through swathes of stained-glass light.
I set her down on dimpled legs
that have already stumbled up
half the staircases of Paris.

I turn to light a votive candle
for an uncle diabetes hacks away at
until he might need only half a casket.

Left alone, Miriam passes
under the velvet stanchion rope
that hangs to keep parishioners at bay,
audience only to the sacred rites of clergy.

Drawn by shafts of light
that fall from high windows,
incense and incandescent candles,
Miriam drifts past the altar.

I stand arrested at the brink
of the great, gold sacristy.
I try to call her back. I call out

but her eyes are already
twin heavens. Slowly, alone,
she starts to twirl through
halos and exaltations of light.

PAIN DE CAMPAGNE

Besancon, France July 1991

Yesterday we found a crooked valley
with one road stitched alongside its river
of rock ledges, boulders atumble and more silver,
more golden coinage tossing there than ever slipped
through fingers in all the counting houses
of the thousanded fiefdoms of Charlemagne's France.

We came upon a restaurant tucked under pines
that served smoked pike, pan-seared perch,
asparagus spears drizzled with cream sauce.

The next morning, back in the city,
dawn slaps the pavement
as I pad toward a tiny bakery
whose windows and ceiling
are blackened by smoke –
have been blackened, been smote
since before the War to End all Wars
ended absolutely nothing.

A half-block from the bakery's store front,
its aroma lifts me off the street.

BESIDE THE LOIRE

Verades, France   May 1991

I go down to the waterline where the river
bends the brass saxophone of its neck
to blow out a ballad begun with mountain glaciers,
drenched by cumulonimbus, funneled between forests,
buffeted under wind, and fed by fields of wheat.

In the gold mead of afternoon
two crickets hop through spiderwort.
A raven is in the top of a willow
whose branches lift in the current.
Downstream the tenor sax begins
to twist and moan against banks.
Then the river slides a slow glissando
under pensioners out to market, schoolchildren,
and lorries that cross stone bridges
in Tours, in Ancenis, in Nantes.

Under sun's blaze, the Loire
flashes the purity of its song.
Around dawn tomorrow, these same
currents will gasp and gurgle
in the heart of the sea.

Where sea crashes against a stone shelf,
amid all those drums, crescendos, trumpet blast,
the high-pitched violins of African winds
that tear the tops off wave crests, whales
in the deep that sound their cellos,
that is where this saxophone
will let out its wild, reed-blown song,
resounding, yet absorbed.

Then Back Out

Florence, Italy   October 2017

I

We pick our way through a spiderweb
of unknown streets to find a cozy B & B
up a staircase in a suburb of tiny shops.
Then realize I have to sail back out
for eggs, milk, cheese and bread.

I get lost in cross-cut streets.
Without warning gusts lift newsprint,
whip flags. Plastic bags shoot past.
In the last edge of gloaming,
buildings loom taller and taller.

I inch my way back as a wicked gale
rips and claws. Foreign rain drills
sideways down alien pavement.
I am lucky to stumble up to our door.

II

We stand and sweat in front
of a Fra Angelico manger scene
that is a chorus of golden grace
hung at the top of a staircase
inside a Renaissance cloister
where Savonarola once wrote.

One chamber of the novitiate
is dedicated to massive, leather songbooks,
gold-embossed tomes of psalms,
chants, madrigals on pages adorned
with peacock plumage, sea foam, dragon flames
and vines woven into the antlers of stags.

Those pages step us back centuries.
Once a choir of altos, tenors, sopranos
left their homes for the archways
and quiet halls of an abbey

set amid tumultuous mountains,
unpredictable weather and the endless
waging of war where they lifted their voices
for as long as song lasted on the page.

VIOLA!

Florence, Italy   October, 2017

We wait twenty minutes
then barely squeeze onto the bus.
Afterwards Renee tells me someone copped a feel,
let fingers linger backside in that blind crush of flesh.

By the time we get to the famous overlook,
sunset is an oiled smolder.
Teens shoot by on skateboards.
Lovers, knots of travelers,
lean over a railing into pine tops.

The next day we stand two hours,
then give up getting into the Uffizi.
For decades, maybe for centuries,
the good people of Florence
have been made tired of the trudge,
trudge, trudge of tourists, sidewalk encounters.
Florentine ears are pained by mangled syllables.
Florentine faces are tired of our faces.

On the next to last night
we happen upon a store
lined with shelves of wine
with one light bulb, no sign.
The proprietor siphons a Tuscan red
from a wall of twenty-gallon jugs
cradled in woven reeds. He corks
our bottle on the spot, asks,
"Is $1.50 too much?"

It is a Montepulciano so delectable
we flick our tongues like serpents
and swear we will be back next year.

LOST IN AN ESCHER PRINT

Rome, Italy   October 2017

We trundle under Rome in subway tunnels
dug through archeological strata where they unearthed
Roman barracks, Christian relics, an Etruscan cemetery.

The tunnels run so deep that two-hundred-foot-tall escalators
are linked one to another, ad nauseam in a series M.C. Escher
might have designed.

The top-most staircases are plain concrete.
I heave. I drag our luggage up onto a street
that gives no clue how to find our hotel.

I hold out a scrap of paper with the address.
Strangers try to help. We speak not that.
They speak not this. Words die on the ear.

When we finally make it, the desk clerk has the face of a
mastiff.

MURMURS AND COOS, COOS AND MURMURS

Rome, Italy   October 2017

Grand legions of pigeons dot the pavement,
flurry beside fountains, swirl by cathedral spires.

The elevator to our hotel starts on a third-floor landing.
The staircase up to that elevator is made of marble,
is worn as saddle leather, scuppered at its center.

No ground left, builders added on skyward,
one structure atop another. History looms above
every street corner, is sculpted into stone cornices.
What's new is many stories high and therefore matters less.

Pigeons wear glory in the shimmer of multi-colored coats.
From their murmurs, from their coos come ancient
benedictions papal bulls no longer have the authority to give.

THE WINE DARK SEA

THE VIOLET CROWNED CITY

The Acropolis, Athens, Greece   September 2017

Arid clarity, wind etched.
Seated at a bistro table
we crane our necks back
toward where we just were –
freedom's cradle amid Doric columns.

Pillars now support blue sky.
A prism band of violet
rests upon mountain peaks
that rim the city round.

An hour ago our shoes crushed
the dust of democracy's birthplace
atop a 450-foot promontory that once
busted up from earth, erupted,
jagged as a lightning bolt.

May Poseidon kiss and calm
stars that wrangle across waves
while our ferry follows its compass
towards Santorini tomorrow night.

Anyone can see that the Gods
feel generous today. Look!
At this very instant,
one of the daughters of Hellas
bears a platter of glass-stems
that hold our sea-dark wines.

BLACK BEACH

Santorini, Greece   September 2017

Shoulder to shoulder
a crowd jostles to watch
the Fira sunset swaddle town, bay, rock
in swells of pink and talcum blue.

I retreat into a church. A matronly woman
bends at the waist to kiss glass
that holds a gilded icon.
Her withered mother does the same.
The next day at dawn
on the black beach
Renee and I are alone
as wind from Cypress
draws a single cloud
into the shape of a harp.

The sun is a host, crimson.
Crimson flames
the crests of waves.

On the street behind us,
a restaurant cracks its shutters.
An old man with cuffs
rolled up over thick socks

sweeps the walk. Cigarette dangled
off lips, he mutters back at the door
where a woman stands –
black skirt, black sweater.

OLIVE ORCHARDS IN SALT MIST

Plakias, Crete   September 2017

I

I would not recommend coming into Heraklion
belched out of the belly of a massive ferry
onto dark streets when your car reservation
has been botched and the night's B & B
is 140 kilometers southeast.

We make it to a bus depot,
predictably soiled, suspect, groddy,
a precinct that belongs to yesterday
where those who have been left behind
shift and stare. We munch what
drops from the vending machine.

Down the coastline to Rethimno
Renee slumps into my shoulder.
In Rethimno, I convince a cabbie
to take a midnight zip across the island.

That highway has been blasted
through mountainsides. The asphalt
makes violent jags beside a gorge
that races on a nib of lightning.

But then, no one ever told us
that a trip to heaven would come easy.

II

If all you want is the finest olives, noblest cheese,
with bread to-die-for and the most salubrious wine
to ever meet each other in front of you at one time –
gathered off shelves at a store
bookended into a row of storefronts
where the checkout girl is the owner's daughter –

and to enjoy these by a window
thrown open to gusts off a sea
framed between arid hills,
olive groves, go to Plakias.
Ask for the innkeeper with three large dogs,
a marble staircase and orange trees.

Ask for the innkeeper with eyes so kind
you realize theirs is the only language
you ever wanted to learn.

AN AFTERNOON LAGS ON

Domnoni, Crete   September 2017

I hope that one more time
I can sit with you
in the shade of tamarind trees
as branches wag in sea wind,
as fronds chatter away.

That we can grow easy
and quiet again together,
watch a turquoise sea
use sunlight to stitch

an afternoon into being
in a place too small
to even call a village.

That one more time
we can be together
the way sea waves
absorb into sand.

POSTCARD WITH RAIN

Amari Valley, Crete   September 2017

You can't breathe and get by any oncoming vehicle
and hold the road at the same instant for all
the treachery of goat paths turned into roads near Frati.

Beside bramble, wattle and daub,
sheep and cattle huddle.
Vistas galore as lightning
licks chasms and crests
that were the first go of Crete
in the range where Zeus was cradled.

Within its zigzag maze, ancient Spilli
holds a score of open shop doors
and one church whose icons blaze gold.
At the city's marbled plaza
a spring spouts out of the mouths
of twenty-five lions sculpted
back when the Venetians
ruled this end of the Mediterranean.
Twice locals come up, bend forward,
fill milk jugs to the brim.

We drive on into even more jagged stuff.
Stop at a well-lit bar in a village suspended
on a cliff's edge. Wizened and draped in black
a grandmother fixes sharp eyes on us. Men
in blue jeans or suit coats smoke, chat.
Lightning blows the sky apart.

YA-YAS

Amari Valley, Crete   September 2017

A Ya-ya can be a bundle of sticks
with a black dress dropped over
or eggplant plump
dolloped into a dark gown.

Ya-yas loiter in doorways, churchyards,
seem immovable at the cafés,
bang pots around their kitchen,
study produce at the marketplace.

Many drape themselves in layers to keep
cold off bones because what warmth
old hearts can pump evaporates
through the parchment of their skin.

Ya-yas wear lacy black
veils of grief, steal along walls.
Ya-yas listen deep, study
every twitch and gesture.

Ya-yas say only what needs to be said
to shape, guide, prune and protect
the branches of their family tree.

Whether laughing or scowling,
a Ya-ya has the eyes of a falcon.

PLEASURE THAT KNOWS NO BOUNDS

Rethimno, Crete   September 2017

You might find the square
of discarded stogies and gum wrappers
where suspended on long chains a dozen swings
hang below a canopy of plane trees.
Each finely painted swing is carved out of tire rubber
into the fantastical shapes of ibis and swans.

You might come upon an eleventh-century
mosque with a single minaret.

Venetians built most of the old quarter
out of stone buffed smooth as marble
to make the city seem glazed.

Streets tilt toward a harbor
protected by a stone seawall.
There are cafés. Sit, sip wine
or sip tea. Try a spanakopita.

Amidst the glitter of waves,
sailboats, pleasure craft
and trawlers swell and bob,
lifted upon the baton
of a drunken maestro.

FLIES APART

Herkalion, Crete   October 2017

At Knossos we see everything:
the bare-breasted sisters, sepulcher jars, aqueducts,
the dolphin room, famous blood-red columns.

In a queue waiting to see how acrobats
once leapt across the backs of bulls,
a Korean woman chatters to her daughter
who wears earbuds.

The guide cannot say
why Knossos was abandoned,
maybe the marauding sea-people.
Did tectonic plates shrug?
Sun, drought could have tortured fields.
until storerooms lay empty, rats ate rats.

On a terrace, a boy squats
in the middle of a puddle.
He ignores his mother's entreaties.
The boy keeps dropping stones
into water where the sky flies apart,
comes back together.

STATE OF GRACE

Samaria Gorge, Crete   September, 2017

I come upon Samaria, two dozen structures
ravaged and abandoned a decade ago
when a flood matchsticked the town.

On the other side of a thundering river,
in cliff's shadow, stands
a walk-in closet of a church
whose door hangs open.

The chapel's meager wall of icons
are as well preserved, as golden
and as carefully rendered as any.
Even on a hot day, dark wood
sunk in shade beside a river
is cool to the touch.

I kneel. I want only what is here,
sanctuary between stone, currents
and the chimes of crickets.

TIMON

Athens, Greece   October 2017

Two thousand cabs throttle, dart and swarm.
We catch the same one twice.

First, after a morning stroll through Plaka where
the Church of the Assumption of the Virgin Mary
has stone-carved windows fourteen centuries old

that let dust motes slowly gyre
through shafts of light to prove
how venerable dust
can become over time.

Then again, three miles northeast
and six hours later under a chalk moon
in front of the National Archeological Museum.

The driver's name is Timon.
Timon keeps family photos
on the cracked foam of his dashboard.
Timon gives us his number,
takes us to the airport the next day.

He has sure, accomplished hands,
had been an electrical engineer
before the economy cratered.
We know Timon's children's names.
He has our address.

"THE BATHHOUSE OF WINDS"

Athens, Greece   October 2017

Spools of wind stroke trees,
work balms into our skin
as we pass through the shadows
of yet another ruin whose pillars
vault into cloudless cyan.

A troubadour from Mali
in multi-colored robes,
slaps a darbuka, sings
beside an Armenian guitarist
whose fingers pluck across complex webs.

For years to come every note
on the CD we buy will sweep us back,

fix us here as if we can float
in the outer shell of a candle flame,
cupped in a gentle warmth that wavers
at the edge of infinity.

TO ISTANBUL ON TURKISH AIRLINES

Istanbul, Turkey   October 2017

Leaving Athens I watch the jet
lift off its shadow, drag
over crags and passes. Shadow
shows how light and wind
arc around this fat arrow.

"That is spirit," I say. "This is what
is left as bulk lifts away. Shade races
over what brilliance brims on the landscape.

When we get over Thrace,
I take a whiskey. Rock
that Turks and Greeks
have battled over since bronze
shields first got hammered.

I take a long drink of scotch whiskey
over ancient Thrace and try to find
what is left of plane's substance
down in that upheaval of stone.

I cannot see a thing until we
pass over the Sea of Marmara.
Shadow reappears as a murky
globule in mist traced over waves.

"That too is spirit traveling at speeds
beyond what sound can reach," I say.
"A quick flivver, soul in flight."

We come in over water.
The jet pivots its wheels down
onto the belly of its shadow again.

FINDING FOOTING

HOW TO GET LOST, ANYWHERE, ANYTIME, FOR NO REASON

Start where streets
that run East-West
radiate off a river so old
it dodders between banks
that loop and rope at their leisure
or off a coastline of Ss and Cs.

Maybe this city's or that's
cross-streets fall across one another
in an abandoned game of pickup sticks.
Follow your feet. Now evening
can tune its orchestra up while
the maestro waits in the wings.

Sunset glazes shop windows.
Doors three inches thick. Faint
hiss of neon. A dog pees. A horn blasts.

That horn blows in a harbor.
Walk that way though alleys become
fly-blown and loose fists of men idle
in front of stoops and broken fence lines.

Come out in a small park freckled
with palm trees. Listen to pigeons
whose language can seem closer
to yours than what the locals mutter.

On the other side is the river.
Its traffic churns sluggishly,
as if already wheeling towards sleep
while stars start to prick black air.

YEARNING

Shreveport, Louisiana   December 2019
It sits unanswered like a half phrase of music on my ear. Barbara
Kingsolver

There is an art to getting lost.
I turn myself over to my feet,

see the way a man in a blue-jean jacket
leans against brick with a beer bottle
in his hand, calls out to buddies,

appreciate what stars shed on buildings
or fields along the railroad tracks,
how a half-moon winks through kudzu.

I watch who comes, who goes,
at what doorway, whether quick or slow,
half-hypnotized or with precise routine

I give up what I am
let Lima, Boston, Shreveport, Crete
show their wares.

Today it is Sunday morning,
almost Christmas.
I am on a sidewalk split
between shadow and sunrise
in shafts, mist and strata

I watch an old couple
feed construction lumber
into a fifty-gallon drum
in a front yard that tilts downward
at an angle like a bird's beak

every corner
a new pang of yearning.

OVER THREE CONTINENTS

As a trucker let me out near Albuquerque,
dusk turned a mountain range mauve.
I was seventeen and knew nothing.
I found a flat spot on a ridge, pushed
small stones aside, uncoiled a bed roll
and went into dreams as coyote built
stairways of howls up toward the stars.

I hired onto boats, worked the rudder,
fixed, let loose and coiled the hawser.
Stared out as wave crests crashed, braced
for the boat to pitch. Years later
I dove through Gulf Stream blue,
held my breath beside anemone.

In the Andes I walked for days,
stumbling and forgetting.
Got beyond severity, care. Bent
to watch a spider link lichen,
flint to scrub. Over a ribbon
of snow, silk net hidden in wind.

Atop mountain passes plants
hardly have enough soil to bud,
flowers tiny as bugs that devour
microbes, survive amidst moss.

I sought seed, womb, fuse,
strove to clean my eyes, fructify
my ears, be stunned in my skin.
By a lake cased in ice, one goose
blew its long horn twice. I was there
when that voice roused the pre-dawn darkness.
I understood what it means to keep going.

TONGUELESS

I helped my cousin raise a broken-winged crow
we found creek side, shivering, almost embryonic.
We splinted its wing with thread and a matchstick.
Nursed it with a dropper for weeks until finally
behind his sloping lawn, by a line of evergreen
planted for windbreak, the bird flapped
tattered wings, disappeared above a cornfield.

Danced in moon-shot surf on the coast
of Flora-Bama where flecks of phosphorus
dazzled under moonlight, excited
in an illuminated dance
beside the one I later married.

Glints in moon-bright granite
above pine, the Appalachian midnight
rock face under which I shivered in
a secondhand sleeping bag beside a creek
whose roar and tumble brightened every star.

Alone in the Peruvian Andes,
two hours' hike past a dirt path where alpaca
were led between isolated villages, a fog
set in overnight. I had left the small lake
where I and some geese bedded, came
to the edge of an impassable precipice,
below which sheep milled by a thatched hut.

I turned back into the vast pre-dawn only
to come face to face, as dense fog parted,
with a strange mountainside, orange under
white wisps – covered with a brush-plant
whose roots drew nourishment
from just rock and air. That is all there was.
Rock, air, fog and a gringo lost in a stone sea.

I have sought solace in stone,
played my flute beneath black sky,
kissed the mouths of sixty women
only to be humbled by endless variation,
tongueless wonder.

A GOOD STEAK IN BANOS, ECUADOR

Banos, Ecuador   May 1979

Always know you are strangers ... in a land far stranger.
~Allan Gurganus

A trail through goat and cow dung
led to thermal baths whose water seeped up
after passing over lava. I sank down.
Twenty feet away a brook roared by.

I went back and forth between these two
the way a French girl told me to do,
called me "Mister American Man."

Back and forth. Extreme heat, furious cold,
until it seemed like knitting needles pierced
deep tissue, organs. Soon there didn't seem much
of anything I knew as me left. Vacant to vast sky,
a ring of mountains, the distant roof tiles of the town.

It was almost two p.m. before I got back to the hotel.
Shops were shuttered for siesta. Still, I found the place.
"Torrinadoes" was legendary along "the Gringo Trail." The
door opened. A bell rang. A thin man told me, "*Se.*" Yes, he
could grill a steak and some potatoes if that is what I wanted.
That is what I wanted, Torrinadoes renowned beef.

The man disappeared. I heard sharp voices, rustling.
He came back with my bottle of *Agua Mineral*. Disappeared.
Louder voices. Furious movement. A sudden gasp. A slap. A
howl. Fast steps.
He came back with his forearm bandaged, in a hasty gauze
drenched with blood. Set a broad knife down on a counter.
"*No hay problema, Senor, uno momentito, no mas,*" he told me. It
was thirty minutes more.

The steak was excellent. I came back that night. I can still call
that soft, sanguine flavor back to my tongue. Thirty-five
years. I went out into foreign streets, cobblestone, sun. Made
my way back to the hotel. Napped. Slowly I mapped out my
return to the U.S.

To what I call home. Though, truth be told,
I am often little more at rest here than
I was there. I write memory, anger, dung, lust.
The writing is what brings me home.

www.ingramcontent.com/pod-product-compliance
Lightning Source LLC
Chambersburg PA
CBHW061659120626
46550CB00003B/1008

* 9 7 9 8 9 9 1 1 9 8 3 9 4 *